SOME MAJOR EVENTS IN WORLD WAR II

THE EUROPEAN THEATER

1939 SEPTEMBER—Germany invades Poland Great Britain, France, Australia, & New Zealand declare war on Germany; Battle of the Atlantic begins. NOVEMBER—Russia invades Finland.

1940 APRIL—Germany invades Denmark & Norway. MAY—Germany invades Belgium, Luxembourg, & The Netherlands; British forces retreat to Dunkirk and escape to England. JUNE—Italy declares war on Britain & France; France surrenders to Germany. JULY—Battle of Britain begins. SEPTEMBER—Italy invades Egypt; Germany, Italy, & Japan form the Axis countries. OCTOBER—Italy invades Greece. NOVEMBER—Battle of Britain over. DECEMBER—Britain attacks Italy in North Africa.

1941 JANUARY—Allies take Tobruk. FEBRUARY—Rommel arrives at Tripoli. APRIL—Germany invades Greece & Yugoslavia. JUNE—Allies are in Syria; Germany invades Russia. JULY—Russia joins Allies. AUGUST—Germans capture Kiev. OCTOBER—Germany reaches Moscow. DECEMBER—Germans retreat from Moscow; Japan attacks Pearl Harbor; United States enters war against Axis nations.

1942 MAY—first British bomber attack on Cologne. JUNE—Germans take Tobruk. SEPTEMBER—Battle of Stalingrad begins. OCTOBER—Battle of El Alamein begins. NOVEMBER—Allies recapture Tobruk; Russians counterattack at Stalingrad.

1943 JANUARY—Allies take Tripoli. FEBRUARY—German troops at Stalingrad surrender. APRIL—revolt of Warsaw Ghetto Jews begins. MAY—German and Italian resistance in North Africa is over; their troops surrender in Tunisia; Warsaw Ghetto revolt is put down by Germany. JULY—allies invade Sicily; Mussolini put in prison. SEPTEMBER—Allies land in Italy; Italians surrender; Germans occupy Rome; Mussolini rescued by Germany. OCTOBER—Allies capture Naples; Italy declares war on Germany. NOVEMBER—Russians recapture Kiev.

1944 JANUARY—Allies land at Anzio. JUNE—Rome falls to Allies; Allies land in Normandy (D-Day). JULY—assassination attempt on Hitler fails. AUGUST—Allies land in southern France. SEPTEMBER—Brussels freed. OCTOBER—Athens liberated. DECEMBER—Battle of the Bulge.

1945 JANUARY—Russians free Warsaw. FEBRUARY—Dresden bombed. APRIL—Americans take Belsen and Buchenwald concentration camps; Russians free Vienna; Russians take over Berlin; Mussolini killed; Hitler commits suicide. MAY—Germany surrenders; Goering captured.

THE PACIFIC THEATER

1940 SEPTEMBER—Japan joins Axis nations Germany & Italy.

1941 APRIL—Russia & Japan sign neutrality pact. DECEMBER—Japanese launch attacks against Pearl Harbor, Hong Kong, the Philippines, & Malaya; United States and Allied nations declare war on Japan; China declares war on Japan, Germany, & Italy; Japan takes over Guam, Wake Island, & Hong Kong; Japan attacks Burma.

1942 JANUARY—Japan takes over Manila; Japan invades Dutch East Indies. FEBRUARY—Japan takes over Singapore; Battle of the Java Sea. APRIL—Japanese overrun Bataan. MAY—Japan takes Mandalay; Allied forces in Philippines surrender to Japan; Japan takes Corregidor; Battle of the Coral Sea. JUNE—Battle of Midway; Japan occupies Aleutian Islands. AUGUST—United States invades Guadalcanal in the Solomon Islands.

1943 FEBRUARY—Guadalcanal taken by U.S. Marines. MARCH—Japanese begin to retreat in China. APRIL—Yamamoto shot down by U.S. Air Force. MAY—U.S. troops take Aleutian Islands back from Japan. JUNE—Allied troops land in New Guinea. NOVEMBER—U.S. Marines invade Bougainville & Tarawa.

1944 FEBRUARY—Truk liberated. JUNE—Saipan attacked by United States. JULY—battle for Guam begins. OCTOBER—U.S. troops invade Philippines; Battle of Leyte Gulf won by Allies.

1945 JANUARY—Luzon taken; Burma Road won back. MARCH—Iwo Jima freed. APRIL—Okinawa attacked by U.S. troops; President Franklin Roosevelt dies; Harry S. Truman becomes president. JUNE—United States takes Okinawa. AUGUST—atomic bomb dropped on Hiroshima; Russia declares war on Japan; atomic bomb dropped on Nagasaki. SEPTEMBER—Japan surrenders.

WORLD AT WAR

Dunkirk

87018

WORLD AT WAR

Dunkirk

By R. Conrad Stein

Consultant:
  Professor Robert L. Messer, Ph.D.
  Department of History
  University of Illinois at Chicago Circle

 CHILDRENS PRESS, CHICAGO

Adolf Hitler watches through field glasses as the Polish capital, Warsaw, falls to his German troops. Soon afterward, the Germans overran Norway and Denmark and then attacked Belgium, Holland, and Luxembourg.

FRONTISPIECE:
British and French troops being evacuated from Dunkirk head across the channel to England.

Library of Congress Cataloging in Publication Data

Stein, R. Conrad.
  Dunkirk.

  (World at war) Includes index.
  Summary: Details the heroic evacuation of Allied troops from the beach at Dunkirk by both British naval ships and civilian craft in June 1940, despite heavy German bombardment.
  1. Dunkerque (France), Battle of, 1940—Juvenile literature. [1. Dunkerque (France), Battle of, 1940. 2. World War, 1939–1945—Campaigns] I. Title. II. Series.
D756.5.D8S7   1982   940.54′21   82-4595
ISBN 0-516-04795-7   AACR2

Copyright © 1982 by Regensteiner Publishing Enterprises, Inc. All rights reserved. Published simultaneously in Canada. Printed in the United States of America.
  2 3 4 5 6 7 8 9 10 R 91 90 89 88 87 86 85 84 83

PICTURE CREDITS:

WIDE WORLD PHOTOS: Cover, pages 8, 9, 11, 12, 13, 15, 16 (right), 18, 19, 23, 27, 29, 34, 39, 40 (bottom), 42
UPI: Pages 4, 6, 16 (left), 21, 24, 28 (bottom), 30, 31, 33, 37, 40 (top), 41, 45, 46
COLOUR LIBRARY INTERNATIONAL: Page 28 (top)
LEN MEENTS (map): Page 22

COVER PHOTO:
The last British troops from Dunkirk arrive in England.

PROJECT EDITOR
Joan Downing
CREATIVE DIRECTOR
Margrit Fiddle

Waiting. Soldiers in war always spend long days and nights waiting. In May, 1940, the war in Europe was nine months old. Yet the Allied soldiers stationed in France had done little but play cards and wait. They waited as the Germans overran Poland, Norway, and Denmark. While those countries fell, hardly a shot was exchanged between German and Allied troops on the Western Front.

The German attack would later be called a *blitzkrieg* (lightning war). But newspapers in Britain called this silent stage of the war *sitzkrieg*.

For soldiers the waiting always ends. On a fine spring morning—May 10, 1940—the German Army struck. The Germans did not attack the British and French lines. Instead they marched into the three neutral countries of Belgium, Holland, and Luxembourg. Those tiny countries were not in the war. In speech after speech, German dictator Adolf Hitler had promised he would leave them alone. The German attack on those neutral countries proved once more that Hitler was a liar.

These German Stuka dive bombers headed for Holland and Belgium in May, 1940.

Over the morning skies of Holland and Belgium came the distant buzzing of high-speed engines. The buzzing soon became a roar. Then the black shapes of German Stuka dive bombers raced out of the clouds. They made a noise so piercing that troops on the ground had to hold their hands over their ears. Some of the Stukas had special sirens attached to their wings to make them sound even more fearsome.

With roars of thunder, the Stukas rained bombs on Belgium and Dutch defensive positions. Then the bombers finally sped back to their bases. And the soldiers heard an even more dreaded sound—the clanking of hundreds of tank treads. The mighty German Army was about to cross yet another country's border.

From the west, French and British soldiers poured into the neutral countries to help with the defense. Many of those soldiers were young, restless after the many months of waiting, and eager to meet their enemy. Those men had no idea they were falling into a German trap.

British soldiers arriving in Belgium to help fight the invading Nazis were welcomed with smiles and flowers.

The Germans hoped to draw the Allied forces into Belgium and Holland with one powerful strike. They planned to encircle them later with an even more powerful strike. The plan was both simple and daring. If warfare can be compared to a football game, the Germans were faking a running play to the right while throwing a touchdown pass to the left.

As the Allies rushed into Belgium and Holland, an immense German army assembled secretly in the forestland to the south. The army was made up of seven armored divisions, three motorized divisions, and forty-five infantry divisions. The tanks and trucks that were lined up on the roads stretched back a hundred miles into the horizon. This force was the greatest concentration of armored might the world had ever seen.

But the Allies had strong forces, too. In manpower, the Allies actually outnumbered the

General von Rundstedt (center) commanded the German army group in France.

Germans two to one. Still, the Germans were sure they would win. They were relying on their daring battle plan.

A cagey old general named von Rundstedt commanded the German army group. His tank columns met little resistance while rolling through the thick forest called the Ardennes. British and French generals had thought the twisting roads of the Ardennes were too primitive to permit the mass movement of modern tanks. But skilled German drivers managed to move their giant machines over the roads.

Above: When bridges had been blown up, German troops used rubber boats to cross rivers during the Nazi invasion of Belgium. Below: British tanks pass through a bomb-shattered street in the little Belgian town of Louvain, which had been attacked by the Germans during the invasion.

This Dutch Fokker airplane was destroyed during the Nazi invasion of Holland.

Meanwhile, Allied armies were reeling backward in Holland and Belgium. In addition to dive bombers and tanks, the Germans attacked with airborne troops. Key bridges and airfields fell to German paratroopers and troops landing in gliders. Near the front in Belgium the Germans even landed a seaplane on a river near a very important bridge. A dozen airborne troops climbed out of the seaplane, overpowered the surprised defenders, and held the bridge for their main force.

To the south, von Rundstedt's huge tank corps broke out of the Ardennes Forest. Ahead of them lay flat farmland. This was perfect country for tanks. Their destination was the English Channel, two hundred miles away. If von Rundstedt could reach the Channel coast while the Allies were still locked in battle in Belgium and Holland, the German Army would be able to trap almost half a million Allied troops.

The opening days of von Rundstedt's race to the sea gave new meaning to the word blitzkrieg. Certainly German forces streaked over France like a bolt of lightning. Tanks, followed by motorized infantry, rolled over the French countryside so quickly that the Allied soldiers had no time to dig in and form lines of defense. The German armored spearhead raced forward with little concern for its flanks. The Germans hoped their air forces would be able to defend their flanks until the infantry could catch up.

Two of Germany's most brilliant
generals, Erwin Rommel (left)
and Heinz Guderian (above) took
part in the German invasion of France.

Participating in this electrifying offensive were
some of Germany's most brilliant generals. One
was Heinz Guderian. He was a tank mastermind
who had organized the structure of German
armored divisions. Another was Erwin Rommel.
He would soon skyrocket to fame as the crafty
"Desert Fox" who commanded the German
forces in North Africa.

British Prime Minister Winston Churchill (above) and French commander General Gamelin (right) met in France on May 16.

Years earlier, German military leaders realized that tanks, motorized infantry, and air power would revolutionize warfare. Many Allied leaders still thought in terms of World War I trench battles. In that bloody war a successful attack was measured by how many yards of ground the attacker gained. Now the German juggernaut rolled forward at the rate of thirty to forty miles each day.

On May 16, British Prime Minister Winston Churchill flew to France to speak with the French commander, General Gamelin. Churchill had been in office for only a few days. On a huge map, Churchill pointed to von Rundstedt's rapidly advancing spearhead. He wondered where the reserve troops were that could be moved in to stop von Rundstedt's tanks.

Speaking in French, Churchill asked General Gamelin, "Where are the strategic reserves?"

The general shook his head sadly and said, "There are none."

"I was dumbfounded," Churchill later wrote. "I admit that this was one of the greatest surprises of my life."

When Churchill returned to England, he made plans to evacuate the Allied troops by sea if they became trapped. He shuddered as he thought of the enormous losses the Allies would suffer during such an evacuation.

With no reserve troops to stop them, the leading German tanks reached the French town of Abbeville on the evening of May 20. Abbeville is a small port on the English Channel. The Germans had reached the sea. The trap had sprung.

At first, the Allied generals decided to fight their way out of the trap. But they argued about when and where to attack the German lines. The arguments delayed the Allied counter-offensive for three days. That was long enough to allow German infantry units to catch up with

This German armored car reached Abbeville, France on May 20, 1940.

The French and Belgian tanks shown above were not able to stop the Germans from taking this small Belgian village.

their tanks and dig in to protect the exposed flanks of the spearhead. The Allies finally launched a weak attack at the town of Arras, but it was beaten back by German infantry.

Then the Allies received another disastrous setback. Belgian King Leopold III realized that his people could hang on no longer. Declaring that "the cause of the Allies is lost," he surrendered his 400,000 soldiers to Germany. This sudden surrender left a huge gap on the Allied front.

Now cornered, the Allied generals agreed to attempt an escape by sea. Their attention turned to a small French city whose name history would never forget—Dunkirk.

But everyone knew that evacuation was a desperate move. The men would have to board ships practically under the barrels of German heavy guns. The skies above Dunkirk would swarm with enemy airplanes. Some defenders would have to hold off German tanks while others made their escape. Because of these dangers, many Allied generals feared that Dunkirk would be a bloodbath.

In England, the enormous job of commanding the rescue operation was given to a British admiral named Bertram Ramsay. He was a quiet, conservative officer who always ran things "by the books." But he knew this evacuation called for desperate measures. The German Army was rapidly closing in on the port of Dunkirk. Ramsay thought he would have only a few days to bring out as many troops as he could. He planned to use everything the navy had, from destroyers to minesweepers. But he

Admiral Bertram Ramsay (left) was chosen to command the Dunkirk rescue operation.

still needed more ships. Then he thought of the hundreds of freighters and small craft that lay at anchor on Britain's east coast. Dunkirk was only forty miles away from the English city of Dover. The freighters and small craft could make the voyage in about six hours.

Quickly, Ramsay picked up the telephone. He ordered the mobilization of every seaworthy ship on the east coast of England. The conservative admiral had dreamed up a new and daring idea.

Over British radio came this unusual announcement: "The Admiralty has made an order to all owners of pleasure craft, fishing boats, or freighters between thirty and one hundred feet in length to report to the Admiralty at Dover."

Dover was the British city closest to Dunkirk. In Dover, Ramsay set up his headquarters in a building that once had housed a diesel-driven dynamo. For that reason, the rescue operation was called "Operation Dynamo."

From all over the English coast, boat owners sailed to Dover. Ramsay soon had all the boats he could use. Certainly they were a curious mixture of boats, but each one of them could carry at least some Allied soldiers.

American radio reporter
Edward R. Murrow (left)
watched the evacuation
boats assemble at Dover.

American radio reporter Edward R. Murrow
stood high above the sea on the famous White
Cliffs of Dover. He watched a very strange
procedure below him. In the choppy water, more
than six hundred civilian boats of all descriptions
had assembled for their first trip to Dunkirk. A
British destroyer cut in among the boats and an
officer barked out instructions through a
megaphone. Finally the officer shouted, "All
right, lads. Let's go to France!" And the
makeshift armada steamed across the channel
toward Dunkirk. Reporting to the United States,
Edward R. Murrow said, "The show
demonstrated again the British genius for
improvisation."

In his headquarters at Dover, Admiral Ramsay nervously listened to radio reports. On all sides the German Army was tightening the noose at Dunkirk. Stukas were pounding the city. The British high command estimated that German tank forces would take Dunkirk in two days. That would give Ramsay the chance to rescue about 45,000 men. Hundreds of thousands more would have to spend the remainder of the war in German prison camps.

This Red Cross van was wrecked by German bombers at Dunkirk.

At sea, the vessels of Operation Dynamo plodded toward Dunkirk. They were a bewildering assortment of crafts—motorized lifeboats, fishing boats, fabulously expensive private yachts, dockyard tugs, fireboats, small freighters, an automobile ferry boat making its very first voyage in the open sea, and even one or two ancient paddle-wheel steamers. Some of these boats could carry only a dozen or so men. Others could rescue as many as a hundred. One ship, the *Brighton Belle*, had taken holiday crowds on excursions to France back in the 1890s. She was part of this strange fleet even though her engines had not been fired up for thirty years.

Manning the boats were crews just as varied as their ships. The men aboard were bankers, schoolteachers, factory workers, farmers, fishermen, doctors, and dentists. London taxi drivers had left their cabs on the streets to answer the call for men to work on the rescue ships. A few boats were crewed by teenaged Sea Scouts whose only previous experience came from taking sailboats on Sunday cruises on the River Thames. Elderly wealthy gentlemen were pressed into service to pilot their own yachts. One of them even took his butler along.

Those English civilians manning the boats of Operation Dynamo had been given a strange wartime request. They had been asked to rescue an army.

On arriving at Dunkirk, the citizen–sailors got their first glimpse of the horrors of modern war. The city was an inferno. A fire-bomb raid had set most of Dunkirk ablaze. The water main had broken and the Dunkirk Fire Brigade could do nothing to put out the roaring flames. One thousand helpless French men and women of the small city were killed during that fire-bomb raid.

In the teeming water, the boats of Operation Dynamo attempted to pick up soldiers. It was a perilous job. Thousands of British and French soldiers waited to be rescued from the docks and the beaches. Above them, German airplanes swept out of the skies to bomb and machine-gun

Thousands of British and French soldiers waited
to be rescued from the docks and beaches of Dunkirk.

Above: Hundreds of troops waded out in the surf of Dunkirk toward the safety of the ships waiting for them. Below: Ships loaded with troops arrive in England.

Property of
Bayport - Blue Point Public Library

Above: Only two of the many small boats of all sorts
and sizes that helped bring French and British troops across
the English Channel from Dunkirk.
Below: Troops arriving at an English port from the trap of Dunkirk.

This wounded British soldier is helped up the gangway of a destroyer during the evacuation of troops from Dunkirk.

the soldiers and the boats. British destroyers and ground antiaircraft guns blasted back at the planes. The thunder of explosions, the whine of bullets, the smoke, the confusion, the wrecked boats, and the dead men floating in the water shocked the Englishmen manning the boats. Dunkirk was more frightening than their most terrible nightmares.

The captain of a small freighter named *Mona's Queen* gave this account of sailing into Dunkirk: "Shells were flying all around us. . . . The ship was riddled with shrapnel. . . . Then we were

Troops leaving Dunkirk on a transport look back at the burning docks.

attacked from the air. A Junkers bomber made a
power dive toward us and dropped five bombs,
but he was off, too, I should say a hundred feet
from us. All this while we were still being
shelled."

When the freighter captain turned to look
toward the city of Dunkirk, he saw great balls of
orange fire and thick clouds of black smoke. He
then looked back at his crewmen: "Owing to the
bombardment, I could see the nerves of some of
my men were badly shaken. I did not feel too
well myself, but I mustered my crew and told

them that Dunkirk was being bombed and was on fire. On being asked if they would volunteer to go in, they did so to a man and I am glad we took off as many [soldiers] as *Mona's Queen* could carry."

After braving the hell of Dunkirk, the boats of Operation Dynamo steamed back to Dover. Their decks were crowded with Allied soldiers. When the troops disembarked, the boats refueled and returned to France. Once more, they found the docks and beaches filled with desperate troops. A sailor named Allan Barrell wrote, "Dawn soon came and we stared and stared at what looked like thousands of sticks on the beach and were amazed to see them turn into moving masses of humanity."

Again the boats loaded up as many troops as they could carry while artillery shells and bombs blasted them. Wrecks of big ships and small lay strewn on the beaches. Some ships were hit and sank while loaded with hundreds of men. Those poor troops splashed about in the near freezing water crying for help. Many of them drowned.

Hundreds of British troops crowded the decks of this rescue
destroyer that brought them from Dunkirk to the safety of England.

British and French soldiers form a human chain to wade through
the water to a rescue ship that was to bring them to England.

On the first day of Operation Dynamo, 7,669 Allied soldiers were brought back to England. The next day the boats rescued 17,804 men. On the third day, that number zoomed to 47,310. Ramsay and the British commanders were both pleased and surprised. They were pleased with the bravery shown by the civilian boat crews. And they were surprised that the Germans had not pressed the attack at Dunkirk with their tanks. Originally, Ramsay thought he would have only two days to evacuate as many men as he could. Now, for some bewildering reason, the Germans were giving him more time.

Again and again the rescue boats returned to Dunkirk. With each trip, they found the beaches black with weary and frightened men. The troops stood in water that was ankle deep, waist deep, and neck deep. Some soldiers even swam out to meet the boats. Crewmen pulled the troops into the small craft. The large ships dropped ladders and the men climbed aboard. The soldiers had to stand nearly on top of each other to squeeze onto the decks.

Day and night the rescue boats labored under a constant barrage of artillery and bombs. Even though the German tanks were silent, their air force and heavy guns bombarded the beaches endlessly. Scores of ships and hundreds of men disappeared under the waters off Dunkirk.

Despite the bombs and shells, Operation Dynamo continued into its fourth, fifth, and sixth days. In England, newspapers were calling the rescue the "Miracle of Dunkirk." But the men at the front saw no miracles. They saw only the fury of war at its bloodiest. One soldier later wrote, "Down on the beach you immediately felt yourself surrounded by a deadly evil atmosphere. A horrible stench of blood and mutilated flesh pervaded the place. There was no escape from it."

For nine days the vessels of Operation Dynamo streamed back and forth over the English Channel carrying men out of war-torn

Dunkirk to the safety of Dover. Each day the British asked each other why the Germans were giving them so much time. Had German tanks attacked the flimsy defensive lines around Dunkirk, the Allies would have been powerless to stop them.

The British did not know that in faraway Berlin, Adolf Hitler had suddenly ordered his tanks to stop when they were on the outskirts of the city of Dunkirk. It was one of his most fateful decisions of World War II.

A wounded soldier receives a drink from a companion after landing safely in England.

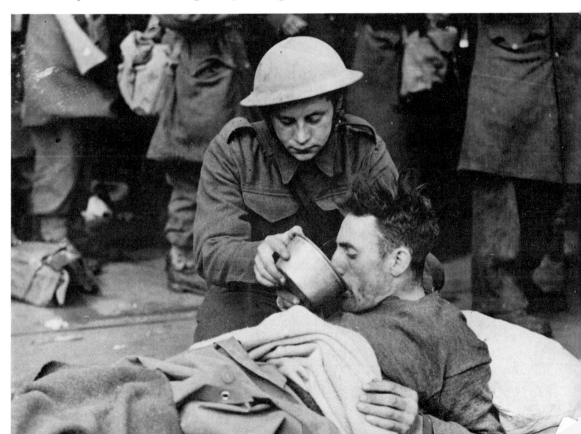

No one knows exactly why Hitler suddenly issued a stop order to his tank commanders. World War II historians offer several explanations for the strange order. One explanation was that Hitler believed his soldiers had become exhausted during their relentless advance. They needed time to rest and resupply. Another explanation involved Hermann Goering. Goering was the chief of the *Luftwaffe*, the German air force. He was upset because the army was getting all the credit for the victory in France. He may have persuaded Hitler to let the Luftwaffe finish off the defenders at Dunkirk so that his branch of the service could get some of the credit. Still another explanation for the stop order was that Hitler did not want to humiliate the British by capturing their entire army. He hoped to make peace with Britain so he would have no enemies to his west when he made his move against Russia.

The stop order infuriated Hitler's generals. Tank mastermind Guderian later wrote that Hitler's order "intervened in the operations in progress, with results which were to have the

German generals, including Halder (left) and Guderian were furious when Hitler ordered his tanks to halt at the outskirts of Dunkirk.

most disastrous influence on the whole future course of the war." German Chief of Staff Halder wrote, "we must now stand by and watch countless thousands of the enemy get away to England right under our noses."

His victories against the western Allies had left Hitler giddy with success. Some men close to him claimed that Hitler had begun to believe he was as great a military genius as Napoleon or Alexander the Great. But certainly Hitler made a major mistake by stopping his tanks at the suburbs of Dunkirk. He would make more blunders, and they would lead to his and his country's ruin.

After their rescue, Allied troops arrived in London
by train (above) and ships of all kinds (below).

Exhausted British sailors, wearing a strange assortment of civilian clothes, line up on the platform of a London railway station after helping evacuate troops from Dunkirk.

In the nine days of Operation Dynamo, 850 vessels under the command of Admiral Ramsay evacuated 338,226 British and French soldiers. The bulk of those men had been brought out by the big ships of the British Navy. But many had been rescued by the brave civilians sailing tugboats, yachts, and freighters. That mixed flotilla plodded steadily back and forth across the English Channel. Their crews ate on the run and hardly paused to sleep at all. The men entered

Soon after taking Dunkirk, the Germans defeated all of France. Below: Germans pass through a destroyed French town.

By June 14, the Germans had reached Paris (above). In Marseilles, the weeping man at right expresses the grief felt by all Frenchmen at the defeat of their regiments.

the bloody waters of Dunkirk a dozen or more times. No one had to tell them when they were getting close. They could tell by the fire and smoke and the distant thunder of explosions. With each trip the men had to overcome terror. A total of 235 Operation Dynamo vessels were sunk by German fire. Two hundred of them were civilian boats. Some 2,000 civilians and British navy men lost their lives during the evacuation.

Hitler finally lifted his stop order and German tanks took Dunkirk on June 4, 1940. The Germans captured 45,000 Allied prisoners. Hundreds of thousands of others were safe in England thanks to the men and vessels of Operation Dynamo.

In western countries, newspapers were calling the evacuation at Dunkirk a victory for the Allies. But British Prime Minister Winston Churchill was quick to point out that "wars are not won by evacuations."

On June 4, while the last troops were wearily climbing off the last transports from Dunkirk, Churchill made a radio broadcast. He delivered what is probably the most famous speech of World War II. At the time of the speech, all of France was falling to the Germans. Many people believed that the Germans were preparing to invade England. It was truly Britain's darkest hour when Churchill proclaimed:

> We shall not flag or fail. We shall go on to the end, we shall fight in France, we shall fight in the seas and oceans, we shall fight with growing confidence and growing strength in the air, we shall defend our island, whatever the cost may be, we shall fight on the beaches, we shall fight on the landing grounds, we shall fight in the fields and in the streets, we shall fight in the hills, we shall never surrender.

Four years after Churchill delivered that famous speech, the Allies stormed back to

Four years after the evacuation of troops from Dunkirk, the Allies stormed back to France on D-Day (above).

France. The war that had caused so much suffering and death to so many millions of people would soon come to an end. Significantly, the first Englishmen to hit the French beaches on D-Day were those same units that had once been rescued from the bloody beaches at Dunkirk.

Relieved to be back in England after their rescue from Dunkirk, returning British troops wave and smile to well-wishers.

Index

Page numbers in boldface type indicate illustrations.

About the Author

Mr. Stein was born and grew up in Chicago. At eighteen he enlisted in the Marine Corps where he served three years. He was a sergeant at discharge. He later received a B.A. in history from the University of Illinois and an M.F.A. from the University of Guanajuato in Mexico.

Although he served in the Marines, Mr. Stein believes that wars are a dreadful waste of human life. He agrees with a statement once uttered by Benjamin Franklin: "There never was a good war or a bad peace." But wars are all too much a part of human history. Mr. Stein hopes that some day there will be no more wars to write about.